There is stunning truth and 'poetry' in Anayah Joi Holilly's *The Angel Code*, that caused me to pause and wonder how the author found the words to help me understand the inexplicable. The answer is in her title; the angels set Anayah on this mission - to transcribe this deep, mysterious and magical material. Our souls, and consequently our lives, will benefit from reading and contemplating the pages of *The Angel Code.* It is compelling and inspiring.

- Sheri Leigh Myers, Author, *It's Too Late to Quit*

Are you ready for the Angel Code? This book is the whispers of Heaven to your heart, bringing the essence of love, helping and guiding you on its wings. Yes, Heaven has wings and they are called angels, here to support you on your journey. This book is profound, yet sweet poetry to the ears. These messages are soft and gentle like the air of God's breath. I could not put this book down as it is filled with delicate treasures, and I wanted to stay in the energy of each word.

- Debbie N Goldberg, Author,

A Divinely Ordered Life Series

THE
ANGEL CODE

Journey Into The Words Whispered To Me

ANAYAH JOI HOLILLY

BALBOA.PRESS

A DIVISION OF HAY HOUSE

Balboa Press books may be ordered through booksellers or by contacting:

Balboa Press
A Division of Hay House
1663 Liberty Drive
Bloomington, IN 47403
www.balboapress.com.au
AU TFN: 1 800 844 925 (Toll Free inside Australia)
AU Local: 0283 107 086 (+61 2 8310 7086 from outside Australia)

Print information available on the last page.

ISBN: 978-1-5043-2285-0 (sc)
ISBN: 978-1-5043-2289-8 (e)

Balboa Press rev. date: 11/13/2020

A little note from me to you,

Throughout *The Angel Code,* you will notice the pro-noun 'she' is interchangeable with 'he'. This is intentional, as the angels remind us we are each a beautiful blend of feminine, and masculine, energies, and that there is balance to be found in remembering, and embracing this.

The Angel Code is non-denominational, its embrace encompasses each and everyone, everywhere, as one family.

Love, Anayah

A note from Anayah on how the last message in this series became the beginning, 15 years and 4 months after receiving the first message.

∞

17 May 2016

I was a bit confused in some of the messages, so I asked the angels "Why do you say 'we', or 'our', when you are speaking to me about 'me/us', not 'you?

The angels answered:
"Because dear child we are never separate,
you are ever without 'us', without 'we'.
We exist not only for you, but in you – as you. We are the breath you breathe, the love your heart beats, the gentle you express. The joy you feel, the pain you experience is not 'felt' by us as you feel it in your body or in your mind, it is however, 'felt' by us as you go through the experiences, much the same way as

a mother feels the pain of childbirth, or a difficult birth of a treasured dream; as a necessary part of the experience, not as the experience itself. As the joy you feel after the journey, after the birthing process, we also feel, and we amplify it for you, as the love we ourselves experience, because of, and in response to – your joy, your love,

your happiness, your achievements. We reflect that – and more – back to you. Each breath you take in peace, love, joy, balance and prosperity, we magnify that, not only back to you, but out into the world *because* of you. Because your creation of these expressions are vibrational aspects of your soul, this is added to the vast pool of universal peace, love, joy and bliss, and you dear one, are a ripple in that pool. Your experiences of joy infuse each ripple – each person – each breath of each person – whether you recognise it or not makes not one speck of difference. You noticing it is merely a reaction – not to be confused with the action itself.

Do you now begin to see, to comprehend, to understand, to gain awareness of, just how important to the entire universe your happiness, well-being, joy, and song truly is? Think on this – ponder at length."

***Creative spelling and mystery
messages. It's all about trust...***

During your relationship with *The Angel Code*, you will notice the angels use of creative spelling and word formation – even 'made-up' words at times. This is entirely intentional on the angels part. Even as they appear as mistakes to us, there is purpose and meaning to each and every word the angels share with us in *The Angel Code*.

You may also notice some messages that seem to make no sense to you at all. Those who need those messages will understand them perfectly, as every word in

The Angel Code is intentional. Trust.

*Should you come across any obvious mistakes, i.e. 'or' instead of 'for', these are mine alone in the transcription process, as are any grammatical errors, for which I apologise in advance.

**I've included a glossary with some of the more unusual words at the end of the book for you.

THE ANGELS MESSAGES BEGAN

and my life changed forever

January 2001

Stating your needs and wants is not considered greed.

You are a wonder of God,

His own beloved child,

of course you should have the best.

Trust in us.

We are here to help you see these things as we do.

All is well

17 January 2001

An easy road to success is not always paved with gold.

Be aware of the road you choose –

always look for the posted signs along the way.

You will always be directed

Trust

Trust

Trust

I am yours no matter the path you choose.

Know this.

Trust this.

Be aware.

∞

ANAYAH JOI HOLILLY

January 2001

All is one – be well, be ready.

Your time is at hand dear one.

Rejoice.

∞

January 2001

Be well, dear one.

Rejoice, have faith, your path is before you.

Another question?

∞

27 February 2001

Take heed, all is well.

Progress runs smoothly – have no fear.

Your time is at hand dear one, the doors are ajar.

Look, listen, and you will find all when the time is right.

Contact, contact, contact.

Note all, ring all bells.

Open your arms,

listen for the soft whispers,

as often the smallest voice carries the loudest message.

Rest – considerable energy will be

needed to carry out your tasks.

Never fear time.

Alaska

Minnesota

Denver Colorado

Whispers

Retreat

Pay attention

Ringing, tones, vibrations, allow all to penetrate.

Listen

Retreat

Retract

All is well, fear not. Be still now.

16 February 2001

Keep at it.

Time is.

Allow.

Breathe.

Make the space.

Godspeed.

No need to rush.

Allow.

Say thank you.

Quiet your mind, a sparrow falls a lonely drop if

you are more concerned with the journey

down rather than the flight.

Allow.

The spirit soars, the physical fears.

Take flight.

You are young yet, be patient as

you would any other child.

The first steps are always the hardest,

feeling fraught with danger.

After a time all things become

possible, joyous, easier, safer.

Magic does happen – allow.

Smile

breathe

await

allow.

Sunshine, heaven sent.

Some parcels are not gifts.

They just are – tools, treasures, it's for you to decide.

ANAYAH JOI HOLILLY

All things have their place, and their jobs.

Tools are a necessity to the carpenter,

for how else does one create a fine piece?

A curve does not appear. it is shaped, a little at a time.

Look at the shavings as they curl.

Like time, these curls unfold as they should.

Allow, shave, curl

Allow, shave, curl

Allow, shave, curl

See the connection?

All is connected.

Feel the connection, for all is one, and one is all.

Abound

Alight

Allow

Your time is at hand dear one.

What is time?

What is a curl of shaving?

A tiny sliver of timber, it becomes nothing

less for the shaving, merely different.

Still whole in its new form –

Perfect

Sublime

Anew

If fear stops the carpenter, what then for the curl?

A new creation denied,

how sad, for all evolves as is intended

from the very beginning.

Flow, rhythm, beauty: are all one.

We are *always* here,

we are *never* apart.

Our sweet child you run and play – we

watch you with sweet abandon,

this is our truth – pleasure, our hope renewed.

A N A Y A H   J O I   H O L I L L Y

An eternal spring from which we

constantly drink – sweet and pure.

All is welcome,

all possibilities – or not, these are your choices,

we do not interfere – it is not our task.

You may – or may not, it is for you to decide.

To grant your own desires is truly possible.

Own it.

Interference is merely fear in action.

All actions are changeable, erasable.

Choose, change, change, choose.

Off you go now – you have the answer.

All is well Cherub – play.

Time is here and now.

Truck

crate

wings

be vigilant, remember the possibilities.

The fork in the road – around the bend,

remember to read all signs.

Language is not a barrier, rather, it

has feathers and can fly.

You are

you are

you are.

Fragrance stirs a memory –

listen!

listen!

listen!

Echoes of the heart – ringing, all tones,

beating of drums signals the arrival.

It's time to listen.

Beating hearts, beating drums, are

they one and the same?

Only time will tell.

An ocean, gently lapping.

Rhythm signals spirit.

Among other things take time to play – to sing.

The smoother flow leaves in its wake abundance,

but only for those who are willing to look.

Think of shifting sands,

as in time, all that passes this way will

once again revisit this place.

It is written.

Do you remember?

Nothing is forgotten – although *all* is forgiven.

Ask for the abundance, for it is already yours.

Look for the wings and take flight.

Keep your pretty ones safe, close to your breast.

The beating of your heart is their guide home.

All tones draw us near.

A bright star shining, winging its way to you now.

Relax, all is in motion.

Allow

nurture

caress

enfold

as we do you.

You are our treasure – sparkle!

17/ February 2001

Be prepared!

Time works well.

Insist/or/insistent.

Patience, slow down, allow us to work.

It our job not yours –

allow

follow.

Are you prepared for the journey?

Time is at hand, heed and hark!

All is well.

Spirit/spirited, stubborn.

One moves along,

the other causes blocks, stops flow, mind debris.

Breathe

breathe

breathe.

A flow, a ribbon of time and space.

Submerge, afloat, the tip of the iceberg – all

is not revealed as you might think.

Wonderment allows healing.

Time passes, it always does.

Come or go – allow or hinder – the process is vital.

As beauty unfolds, the eye beholds, and allows,

each and every wonder to be remarkable

for their very own sake –

for their very own sake –

not to be compared to any other, each

a wonder in its own right.

As it is with all God's wonders – the

breath *is* the possibility –

anew – unfurled

unbound by the restrictions that also

accompany each new possibility.

As you see them, we see the whole –

to be, or not,

you can easily constrict even the flow of time.

Be Still

allow

accept.

The tide turns as it should.

All in time

it's own time

enjoy the journey, it is it's own.

Remember the passing, the milestones, all lessons.

Heed all bells, the ringing is for you,

ANAYAH JOI HOLILLY

allow all tones, vibrations to sing within your soul.

Pure tones are healing to the spirit as well as the body,

just listen

revelations are sometimes whispered.

It is best and advisable to clear the way for news to arrive.

Rest, revise.

A circle. A cross the room – ever widening

ever allowing the process of strengthening the bonds

that allow growth and development anew.

Too many questions

slow down

in time.

Just be – relax, don't hurry – so much to be missed.

A small loss or a grieving,

who's to know the difference when

the hurry is advanced –

blinded by the footsteps, eyes downcast –

rainbows do not occur on the ground.

Glance above the horizon for that is where you are going.

Wings will be needed, and provided, for those that allow.

The dance has its own music – feel it, allow it,

it takes place whether you do, or not –

it is not dependent on you or your presence.

It is – visit, or turn away – your choice.

Be aware.

Be still.

For some things, the choosing is done while

you are busy living a life of your choosing,

but not of your capabilities.

You do think so small – what a shame –

your choice after all.

Weep

rejoice

all of your choosing.

Choose again, it is easy, allowable.

Choice: a cross to bear, a garland to wear –

yours for the asking. You *must* ask

always,

you do anyway, be *aware,* you are already choosing –

choose right. Little footsteps echo.

∞

27 February 2001

A circle never ending; a continuing line

of light, never to be extinguished.

A line of infinite possibilities:

of hope

of truth

of prayer

available always, and in every way accessible.

Boundless. An arc of immense power –

pure bliss for those who choose to access it – us.

We are glad tidings, bringing forth a great joy,

a love that has no limitations – pure bliss.

Like mist we rise and float.

Be at peace.

Know no fear, your time is at hand dear one.

This too is limitless.

An energy bringing forth abundance,

a shining star, for all to see, and be

guided by its shining light.

Youth – ah - such a wondrous gift –

not confined to the body –

the soul, the joys of true wonderment,

sparkles, shines, gives hope, quenches all thirst.

No need for you to go hungry,

a constant source of nourishment is

always being supplied to you.

Oh, if only you would allow yourself

to nurse upon the divine and pure light of love –

peace is always ready to blanket you

Sebastian – Trinity – the ringing of the bells

tones – vibrations – carry forth our message.

Allow – absorb.

It is simple, it always is.

Just choose – then do.

No need for cross purposes, this is

strictly a human conditioning –

align

alight

allow.

A young girl wearing flowers in her hair,

soft curls misting about her face – the

truth can be seen here –

look – look – look – do you see?

Do you allow it to dawn upon you?

She is truly Gods wonder girl –

wonder filled – wonderful,

truly she is you Cherub, go forth and be free –

for freedom is truly yours for the taking.

Blessings to you.

A tender spirit

as with the unfurling of a rose bud,

so too is your tender heart.

Allow,

accept,

enrich.

I have no name. I am truth – wisdom.

Beauty abounds,

alight

allow

shine.

Peaches – my name is Peaches.

This name is for you – my gift to you.

Sweet, abounding sweetness.

Fare well.

The line of sight – your world deviate –

nothing is ever so straightforward as

to have no other possibilities –

no other wonders to be discovered.

All is needed, is the willingness to follow

guidance as a small child is willing to,

so should you – important, important, important!

Listen/hark/heed

Allow now, your time is at hand dear one.

Don't try to hurry the process –

process is

process is

process is.

Allow.

All roads travelled bring us closer, to God –

God our loving father – abundance of course!

Of course – think on this.

Of. Course.

What is the course?

Plot your course by the words spoken

to you in the stillness.

As the stars guide – so of course –

ponder on this at length – answers

await, revelations abound.

You are on your way. Have no fear, we assist.

Ah … hear the stillness,

feel its comfort,

that is us.

Be well

Be true

Be free

it is allowable.

Let yourself go, flow –

as All does, so shall you,

your mighty spirit is the truth, the magic, of it all!!

Keep your hands focused –

ANAYAH JOI HOLILLY

the source –

allow all vibrations to ring clear and

long – for this is for all.

Peace be with you – for it is and it is.

28 February 2001

Arise dear one, hark.

Allow wisdom – seek truth.

Clear the way, a journey begins.

As a Phoenix, arise from your ashes.

Wisdom is not an easy pathway child,

allow yourself room for growth,

for all growth requires change and development.

Arise – Anew – Awareness comes.

We are here, we hear all – judge not –

we leave that to you – your right,

your dimension, your gift.

It is not for us to decide.

Peace is here, it is within you all.

Access

Access

Access

This is the key.

Godspeed.

Choice is growth, choice speeds growth.

Time is – allow it, nurture its flow and

the rewards are many – a lesson.

13 March 2001

Stay well, stay safe, stay in touch.

Leafy green, in time, in tune, in touch.

March 2001

Awareness carries with it responsibilities.

Hark, heed, around the corner lies awareness.

For you, now is here, and now awareness is arriving.

Living is a life of your own choosing, a valid choice,

for you make your own way.

A winding track, worth all the bumps, turns.

Break downs are inevitable – par for the course.

Remember a sparrow falls? [16 February 2001]

Remember, always remember

the journey is

the journey is

ah… the journey, what a wonderful time.

We hear, we see, we know.

We offer assistance only, it is for the asking –

that is for you too.

Time is no barrier.

Persist.

Cease communications.

Open, allow, arrival is imminent.

Unbound your hands, allow the arrival of news.

The way is now clear, open the channels,

help is at hand dear one.

Allow the flow as Rhythm.

Open the channels, clear the desks, for truly

a smile is beaming its way on to you now.

Be patient, get ready, prepare for the

arrival as you would a guest.

Be properly prepared for the arrival,

time is at hand dear one.

Be still now, have faith, for what

you ask so shall it be given.

Time, allow all to penetrate.

From the well fill your cup till overflowing,

and drink deeply from

the Source of all good will, for it is yours, a gift for you.

Light the way, mark the course granted.

Tis time now, be ready, be well, accept.

Look into the clear waters as you would a mirror,

for the reflections cast are true and reliable.

Dark hair, white smile beams, radiant,

you will know him, his truth is welcome.

Loving arms to enfold you,

gentle dancing eyes to light the way home.

A true course – plot your course,

he is here waiting patiently in honour of truth.

Seek to find all, stay on course, shine brightly,

beam – your radiance is his guide

1 April 2001

Resistance is use less.

Plot your course, mark the way for

to you now comes a gift,

our gift to you. The time is here, at hand, at last,

for your pleas have indeed been heard, and answered.

Among other things, take time to play,

for the joyful path is as important as bread is.

Sate your hunger

for it is – it just is –

food for the body, food for the soul,

they are indeed one and the same child.

Know this, trust, it is a time of jubilation.

Be aware, as always, for it is wise

to know your limitations,

and too, the limitations of others.

These limits are not meant to stop you,

merely recognise them for what they are –

new pathways that need exploring,

new courses to be plotted.

Awareness is it is not to be forsaken.

Is a ruby found already cut and polished,

or is it rough,

for some, not recognised for its true

value, overlooked so easily.

Is it any less valuable in its rough form

to you, those who truly see?

We are all like these gems,

our shape changes and grows more refined as

the cloth of love and light is offered to smooth our edges.

With careful and considered polishing and trimming,

the true inner beauty is exposed.

It was there all the while,

there, for those who would see beyond the surface.

Fear not precious one,

your gem stone has already undergone

much of the process we speak of.

Be as the polishing cloth,

be ever rhythmical, let the flow smooth the way.

Allow the course to flow as it has been

plotted – the rough with the smooth.

Abrade

Abridge

Abide

Your time truly is here – it's for you, the

decision is yours, it always is.

4 April 2001

It is a wondrous and true beauty –

a spark, a miracle, bonds forged, a joyous event!

Miracles do occur,

daily, events take place, meetings transpire,

a glance, a touch, a word spoken,

these things and more, events that come together.

A symphony, like cascading water in a waterfall –

majestic, yet made up of tiny individual drops,

each a beauty in its own right.

Separate, designed by the hand of God,

yet necessary, and in need of the

company of others of its kind.

Alone, it withers and disappears unnoticed,

together, part of the total experience, by Divine right,

for a right it is, to be part of a greater experience,

a true and valuable part of the whole, of its own kind;

separate, individual, but belonging to

the greater scheme of things.

This is as it is intended – always has

been from the very beginning.

A wondrous divine dance.

Let the rhythm take you, sweep you along in its path –

for the pathways are true and straight.

Strength lies in the flow –

life, cycle, abundance.

Abundance - think on this.

Adapt – it is your nature – your strength.

Take heart, we guide you, we have the plan, it is in motion.

The motion sways, Rhythm – sway with it,

feel its beauty, its abundance, for strength lies in this flow.

We are here, we three, we watch, we listen, we see.

Direction is possible – cast yourself to the rhythm,

be full of grace, be true, it comes, the time is near,

hark

heed

be well

follow

direction is always available, as are we.

Your turn now, let the dance begin.

Serenade as you would whisper the words, gently, gently –

like the flutter of wings, so is the beating of hearts.

ANAYAH JOI HOLILLY

This is good and true,

allow all truth to be told, to be heard, hold back nothing –

for this journey honour thy Father.

Your path is true and straight, the course is true.

Let love be allowed to grow, gently

nurturing, sweet whisperings

Take care, cause not to bruise with haste.

You know this – remember it.

Hark, heed, adhere.

Grace, beauty, await.

It is worth patience, grant this,

for your time ahead needs care full consideration.

You have a new horizon – soar.

The warm currents are there to greet you,

spread your wings and take flight –

it is but a leap of faith anyway – as is all.

What has gone before allow to rest –

open all doors, fling them wide, embrace

the gift, it is yours, truly.

Time is of the essence – all its beauty to unfold –

act in haste and bruising will occur.

To bruise is to cause harm, damage.

Like the parting of curtains, greet

the dawn with new eyes.

It is a joyful event to come – allow the blessings – let go –

soft hands, warm heart, gentle ways,

time is needed for the healing to take place.

Time is – time is – that is all – it is!

Nothing more – nor less, it just is.

Allow it, enfold, your kindred spirit, he is here

∞

Good Friday April 13 2001

Beauty abound, joy is precious, a gift to you,

yours for the taking – it is as it should be.

Alight, Abound, your time is here and now, embrace the joy.

ANAYAH JOI HOLILLY

News is at hand dear one, we send to you a chorus,

the seed, its tender shoot, warmed by the sun, (Son)

as is all, for all is here and now.

Plant, reap, the cycle of life, of growth, it

is eternal, no matter its form, it is.

Scatter your seeds, nurture, warm as the

sun – your love, a light, a glow.

A gentle hand is the hand of God – feel its

touch– a constant source of light.

Light governs the way, allow the journey,

this gift is precious, for you, and only you,

for, no other can walk your path, choose your way.

These choices, these gifts, never

underestimate the power of choice,

the grace, the beauty that choice is,

the love these gifts were bestowed with,

for you, for you all, taken for granted, it's never too late.

∞

1 May 2001

Possibilities are Choices – the ebb

and flow grow and change.

These gifts come to you as growth, as choice anew.

Your faith – test its bounds, feel its strength, enrich –

encircled in its power, possibilities abound.

Bide your time, for matters, resolution

winds its way to you –

conclusions are but new beginnings anyway.

As the mighty oak comes from but a seed,

so the seed comes from the oak,

the circle of renewal, it's life force.

Allow time, growth – the cycle needs time.

Not all is apparent –

trust,

allow

have faith

ANAYAH JOI HOLILLY

for what else is there?

How else did you find your way here?

You know the answers to your questions,

you need not fear time.

Be generous of spirit

be kind of heart

gentle in your ways

let your spirit be your guide.

You know the path, the true course, the way home.

Follow your path, the footing is sure and

true, however you may stumble –

pick yourself up, cast your eyes to the horizon, seek truth.

Majesty awaits – the winding path leads you home.

Follow it, stay on course, stay true, stay well, stay whole.

Remember the bells, they ring for you,

their tones are nourishment for the soul and body alike.

2 May 2001

Seek truth, acceptance of self and of others.

When we seek self acceptance, we

must also seek, and accept,

acceptance of others.

Ask for guidance – also, remember to say thank you.

Bitterness grows when acceptance

is not practised nor desired.

Desire knows many forms – open your heart to them,

let them find a home to reside in.

Open yourself to the possibilities, for this is growth.

Know this, trust this, honour this.

Your path is clear, seek it.

Open not only your heart and mind, but too your eyes.

Be available to new encounters of the spirit.

Let love linger, let hope flourish, let faith prosper,

for here lies a wondrous journey, yours for the taking.

Ride the crest of the wave, for here is

now, and here is where you belong.

ANAYAH JOI HOLILLY

It is good, it is for you.

Little footsteps echo.

Ring the bells, they are for you, a gift, a treasure.

In time all will become clear.

Trust

Allow

Alight

Align

Share in this truth – it is do-able, affordable.

Hope floats, love soars.

Transcend fear, limit not your possibilities –

your time here is now.

Be in the now, for here lies all truth, hope.

11 May 2001

The possibilities are endless.

As the tides, so too, comes to you

change, growth, renewal.

As you feel its pull on you, it's ebb

and flow, it's give and take,

so should you experience anew each

possibility, each new gift.

Open your arms to their gifts, for gifts they are –

to you

for you

with, or without you.

Join the chorus, raise your voice.

Wing your way, still your mind, for

it too has a flow, a rhythm.

Find it, seek, always seek –

for in this Journey lies the answers for

which you were born to discover.

ANAYAH JOI HOLILLY

The treasure is hidden, but it is there,

accessible always for those who wish it.

∞

28 May 2001

Hark.

Ahead lies your true course, the way

becomes clear, the time draws nearer –

your steps await the commands.

Insist, or insistent voices ring, echo truth.

Words abound, the ringing is for you.

Raise your voice, tis your turn to

sing. Pure tones reflect truth.

The shadows cast are not to be denied,

a new truth awaits discovery,

detection is near for those who seek.

The search is the dance – let the dance unfold as it should,

offer not resistance, for resistance brings with it ill will, a conflict of purpose.

Like the arrow, keep your course true.

Truth and faith, a potent combination.

Mark time, allow the journey its course and conclusion.

Along the way the passage of time may cause concern.

Do not be alarmed, all points have been marked,

check them as you pass, remember to always take note.

Always consider the wisdom of your actions,

before, during, after.

All are valuable, as truth lies within.

Consider this, consider that, consider all.

Discount nothing, as truth is revealed through diligence.

With truth comes peace – a lightness of spirit.

29 May 2001

Cease and desist!

Allow the flow and rhythm to weave

their way through the tangle you find yourself in –

nothing can be gained from the

battering of souls, of wills.

Be kind.

Allow yourself the grace and beauty

only found in the quiet moments

where your two minds can become aligned.

Nothing will be gained through this

twisted path you are now on.

Allow the gentle side to emerge, to

become your true guide.

Resistance leads only toward more

tangled weaving of hurt and pain.

Tis not always evident, nor is it easy,

but know that the path is always

just beyond your conscious realm, always

available for those seeking its true course.

Remember a sparrow falls? [16 February 2001]

Is this not the same thing?

Search your true motives, be not afraid of your truth.

The bells ring for you – the light shines,

cast it toward your darker moments,

allow truth to be your true and only guide.

Your time will come.

Patience is not always accessible, not always available.

Chide not yourself, rather, learn, listen, become still.

It is. It is.

The true course is often rough, seemingly treacherous,

easily mistaken for peril,

when in fact, the storm always brings

with it calm, peace, quiet.

First the storm, then the quiet.

It is the way of it after all.

One without the other is not the way of it.

ANAYAH JOI HOLILLY

Ponder this at length and it becomes obvious to all.

Perfection is so often mistaken for worth,

when in fact it does not exist at all on the human plane.

Peace would be better suited as your intention.

Calm the waters, soothe the soul, become willing, pliable.

This is a more worthy use of your time and energy.

Become willing to alter your perception,

other areas need your attention in order to flourish.

Let kindness be your guide and your

true motivation will be revealed.

All through truth.

This is the key – use it to unlock the hidden pathways,

to gain access to your destiny, destination.

3 June 2001

Let patience be your guide home.

Your course is true - follow it faithfully home.

Along the way your tasks will be revealed to you.

Be aware, be open to the possibilities as

they unfold themselves before you.

Often, time is mysterious to you,

know this for its own truth,

let all be revealed to you in its proper sequence.

All in time, as time allows, for it is to be so.

Along the way, stop, be aware of your true motivation,

your purpose will become clearer.

Is it worthy of your true self, of your time and energy?

Think on this.

Your time, and your life energy.

These are precious, and should be considered so

for where are they born from, and what is their duration?

Think on this.

ANAYAH JOI HOLILLY

Is this truly worthy of the gift?

Tis given freely its true, still, choose wisely.

Become

Become

Accept

Allow

Say thank you

Nothing comes your way by accident.

Realise this, for this too is a gift.

Let your spirit soar – smile in the face of God.

8 June 2001

Sometimes, the path we choose may convey

the need to shorten our footsteps.

With each new footfall comes the opportunity

to observe ourselves in context.

We do not always take the time, or

the opportunity, to do so.

The images cast offer insight.

The shadows cast are often bathed with insight

if only we would allow the light of

truth to light the corners,

if only we would allow our glance to linger long enough

to discover the hidden truths held there in the shadows.

A darkened truth is truth nonetheless.

Whether we choose to see, or not,

is of course, part of the journey, part of the discovery.

Painful

Enchanting

Enlightening

Who's to know unless the veil of fear is lifted.

Fear becomes as a stone in the shallows,

there, visible, accepted.

Reach in and remove the stone, see what lies beneath,

what squirms in the sudden light of day.

Examine the findings, allow them to be what they are,

then, as is their way, allow them to disperse.

ANAYAH JOI HOLILLY

For some things, the dark is essential

to their very survival.

Not all can live and prosper in the light.

You are free to choose.

Remember this, exercise this right with

care, and attention to detail,

for it is in the detail that sometimes truth is revealed,

for truth is about what is, as it is.

It is not always expected, nor recognised in its true form.

Be true

Be well

11 June 2001

Shadows dance.

Abundance falls at your feet.

Tis time pretty one, your time draws near.

Light the lamps, place them in the windows.

A gentle soul draws near.

Allow this time of discovery, for in this time,

treasures are uncovered and exposed to the light.

Sway in time, the music beats in time,

for in time, comes time.

Coax the rhythm, for at times a shyness is evident.

Respect all, for all has its own place and time to be heard.

A gentle hand is needed to stroke the

ruffled feathers of a startled bird.

The pounding of the frightened heart needs time to become

accustomed to its new environment,

to decide whether to take flight, or to stay...

Tis a momentous occasion, this time of decision-making.

With choice comes responsibility,

new challenges to discover.

As the grass grows, so too, the winds

that brings the seeds of change –

ANAYAH JOI HOLILLY

there is not one without the other.

Allow the natural course of events to take its shape –

do not try to mould it to your own will.

Do you know to where the sparrow flies?

The arrangements are not for you

to concern yourself with –

rather, grant yourself the gift of peace,

and allow us to move as we are meant to.

The time and place are not relevant at this time.

All in its proper sequence, the order of

events are not your concern.

Be as the seed – float upon the

current to your new home,

your destination will become

apparent to you as it should.

When the current becomes still, your time

and place will become clear to you.

All as is necessary.

No need for fear, as it is intended, so shall it be.

The mighty ocean knows no fear, nor shall you.

Be at peace, feel its currents, the ebb and pull of its tides –

it shall be so, and it shall be so.

Give and take – all returns to the Source.

This is the way of it,

its own truth told through one and all,

it sings for you, for you all,

father and Son – the message is clear, let

it come to you – no need to seek.

Ponder its message, listen in the silence,

hear the truth, for it is there.

Just ask and it will be revealed to you,

perhaps a little at a time,

don't be impatient, it brings to you

a time honoured treasure.

Be open to it,

be still

await

allow

alight.

Soon, you will see.

Become ready, become willing to accept.

Ask

Always ask for help.

Be still now.

∞

14 June 2001

Truth.

Keep it.

Seek it.

Tell it.

Be ever vigilant, seek to become its guardian.

Whispers carry to you glad tidings, a

message of hope, a seed of renewal.

A time of celebration awaits, beckons.

Greet it with outstretched arms.

Enfold, enrich, enjoy.

The news comes to you, for you.

It is welcome, it is time, a little at a time.

Revelations abound, their sweetness

a balm to your parched soul –

a sweetness to rival all.

Be aware of the time, keep your eyes cast this way and that,

let nothing escape your attention,

for it is revealed in the detail, in the lack of.

Let the sweetness guide you on,

think as you would, not as you might.

Check on the reflections,

see beyond the offered hand to the eye beyond,

what do you see, for there lies the true

motivation and spirit of the thing –

a peace not true nor felt.

Be wise, guard your wisdom well.

The clock is ticking, listen to its message, it is for you.

ANAYAH JOI HOLILLY

Reflect upon the intentions, find the truth

for it is always there – near or far.

∞

19 June 2001

The spirit flows, its bends and turns not visible to the eye.

Its course often a mystery to you.

As is often the way, the mysteries unfolds a little at a time.

Think of the parable, as it too has the

same way of unfolding before you.

Sometimes, understanding is instant,

other times its meaning dawns upon you bit by bit.

Do you see? Is our message clear to you?

Remember, always ask, always seek our assistance –

please, we need your permission to do our work,

it is not so straightforward as it may seem.

You have in you your own river, with its own flow.

We do not stem its flow, nor do we channel its waters.

It is for you to decide, for you to choose.

No need to wonder, for you only need

ask for the answers you seek.

∞

20 June 2001

The bond has indeed been forged, its

strength lies in its gentle curves,

its ties are loving, truly, a token of all that is possible.

Awaken, your time of slumber has past.

Loving ties, gentle though they are, their grip is true,

you know this already, we only speak to

you of truths already known to you.

Patience is now the way; be true, be ready,

allow yourself the time, for in time

you will find your way home.

Your destination is clear, you know this to be so –

for truly it is so, and so it is now, for you.

ANAYAH JOI HOLILLY

Your time is indeed at hand dear one –

as promised, at hand, at last.

Smile, your love awaits.

Be ready, be willing, be available to

the natural flow of events –

for it is in the flow that truth is revealed.

Your spirit sings, the notes are pure, the tone resonates.

Listen.

Be prepared, you are not yet ready, do as you must –

be aware of time, it marches on

regardless of the drummer.

Pack

unpack

crate

wings

truck.

It is coming towards you now – in the distance still,

winding its way on to you, steadily onward.

Time will reveal, the intention is

clear – will become clear.

As time allows, all things align.

Breathe, allow the process.

Remember, process is, process is, process is vital to all,

connected to the spirit and flow of all.

As your time draws near be aware, vigilance

is necessary to your outcome –

be ready, be willing, take all news with calm,

intentions become apparent as the journey progresses.

Cast a stone – read the ripples as they spread.

Notice not only reactions, but look too for

the truths revealed unintentionally

by those who seek to dispel harmony.

It is an ill wind that blows,

for not all share in your happiness.

Harm is sometimes caused by haste –

choose your time, be true, and all will prevail to the good.

You need not fear however, for truth will conquer

and become apparent as time passes.

Be willing to prevail

be honourable

be quiet

be true

as in truth comes your home, your heart.

The circle continues, travel by its

course ever onward, ever true.

Plot your course by this, and be

guided by the one who shines.

You will know all as it becomes necessary.

Are you ready?

Prepare for the journey ahead, be willing,

as it is in this state of willingness

that truth is shown and the path becomes clear to you.

All will be well.

Trust

Trust

Trust

We are here, we will guide your steps.

Ask

Ask

Ask

Don't be afraid Cherub, all is well.

Let our words be your guide.

All is possible for those willing to believe.

Belief brings with it all roads, all maps –

all directions become clear,

all paths lead home.

Abundance awaits – be willing to

embrace this abundance,

never lose sight of this truth.

Sometimes, perspective looses shape –

define – definition adds substance.

As one defines, one shapes thoughts

previously hidden from view.

Part the mist, it is there, waiting to

be claimed like a lost child,

needing to be taken, and enfolded, in

the arms of loving acceptance –

claimed

acknowledged

accepted

home.

Home at last where it belongs –

with you.

∞

23 June 2001

Raise your voice – sing aloud.

To share one's happiness is to truly

receive the gifts we bring,

to know the meaning of abundance,

for, it is in offering your voice

to the voices of others that a choir is born.

Let the melody play, let the notes ring pure and long.

Linger awhile, feel the strings play their

music, for the tones allow healing.

The time has come for you to stretch

your wings, take flight,

soar, become all that you are.

Shelter not in the shadows, step forth into the Son.

Know your path, for surely, now is your time.

Arrive, depart – are they not the same?

Merely notice from where you are

standing which it is for you –

see, the platforms offer points from

which to begin your journey,

and so too, a place to rest awhile,

for sometimes the spirit grows weary,

in need of rest and solace.

The Journey brings with it times of trial, times of anxiety.

Let these two go hand in hand, for not

only are they companions,

ANAYAH JOI HOLILLY

but each in need of the other to allow

the messages of fear to be heard.

In fear you may find a friend,

for the face that turns toward you

reflects truth – hidden it's true...

cast your doubts aside, allow the light of fear

to wash toward the reef, for beyond the jagged rocks of

self doubt, self pity, and unloving-ness

for your own precious child,

lies a safe harbour, where the warm waters of self love,

acceptance, and a gentle heart,

beat in time with our own –

a dance all our own, of our own, ours alone –

for each and every heartbeat is an

affirmation of your own true self,

of your own, wondernesss, unique, sublime –

a creation of magnificence, not to be questioned, abandoned.

Align your true beauty with an acceptance

of what is your own true gift…yourself.

Your very own self, for there is no other –

you alone are the one true creation that is you.

Do you not see the truth of this – must you turn away?

Deny this even to your Father, your Creator?

From where are you born, and to where shall you travel...

one foot follows the other – this is not coincidence.

The plan is obvious to you –

why must its true beauty be lost in questions, in fear?

Think on this, the Plan is simple, no

need to complicate matters.

You have the ability – your denial changes nothing –

it merely burdens you by its weight.

Offer it up, allow its removal.

Release it to joy,

be joyous

joyful

jubilant.

This is the way –

the platform for all arrivals and

departures – for one and all.

And as it is, it is so.

Sow and reap – a time honoured way.

Weigh this patiently, for hurry is

often mistaken for industry.

Rest.

Revive your flagging spirits, fan the embers of hope.

Let your faith become a beacon.

Shine brightly, cast your radiance wide.

Light the corners, ring the bells –

let the tones carry your message to all who would hear,

the song needs the company of many voices.

Its melody is sweet, let it ring long and true.

You are the instigator of your own tune – allow

its harmony to play upon your ears.

Listen!

Listen!

Listen!

Do you hear it?

Do you seek to understand its message to you?

It is for you, and you alone, this message.

Invite clarity into your life.

Allow yourself to become peaceful.

Peace – full.

Is it not obvious that this is to be your intention?

Knock on the door – keep knocking.

The ears that hear are bound to hear, if the

notes of your knocking remain true.

Don't give up, nor give in.

Stay true – stay focused on the outcome you seek.

You are on your platform;

choose your method of transport in order

to arrive at your desired destination.

There are always ports of call along the way.

Visit, learn, keep your perspective focused.

Change is only a way of seeing a thing after all.

See all, ponder much.

The bells are for you – listen.

Remember this: arrival times are subject to change.

Go with this flow, and you arrive in

harmony with your surroundings,

refreshed and in the spirit with which you must stay

in order to do the thing that is your

journey and destination.

You are free to choose, as always.

Choose well, stay close to the Source.

Stay true, be not available to be

swayed by those who would –

this is for you – you are welcome.

Sing now, your voice is true and strong.

Feel its vibration ring long and loud, sweet and clear –

the music will be provided as is

necessary for the outcome.

Sing sweetly, Angel Tones, Angel Songs,

for those willing to hear, a festival for the heart and soul,

rejoice through body and soul alike.

∞

25 June 2001

Your quest is one of greater depth

than you may at first realise.

Of course, it always is.

Fear is not to be feared, rather, it is your friend,

and truly, your questions are born from this place,

they reside in its murky waters, its darkened corners,

here you will find the waiting room

for all your unopened gifts.

Set them free – all of them,

escape from your muddy depths.

Your fear can set you free, for here live the questions

in need of not only answers, but of your loving arms.

Wrap yourself in the quilt of acceptance.

From this place all things are indeed

possible

probable

allowed

easy.

Find your still place, visit often,

become a welcome tenant.

Does your fear not offer you the opportunities you seek?

Look.

Search.

Listen.

The answers are hidden here.

Do not mistake your feelings of fear

for that which it is not,

do not expect to proceed without fear,

for it is in fear that often we

find the key to our hidden resources.

We offer you that which is yours already.

The choir is always in need of voices.

Many voices ring.

Clear the way, for room will be needed for

the word to travel – as travel it must.

Many hearts beat in time with your own.

Just write.

Do not try to leap ahead of yourself –

the steps unfold as necessary.

Now is not the time – second guessing

is not in your best interest.

Be still, find your own company –

seek to become open to direction.

30 June 2001

Your time draws near.

Rest awhile, all is not lost to you.

For now, be alone, be available to yourself alone.

Quiet moments bring solace.

Along the way, gift yourself kindness.

Rest your burdens from time to time,

as no shoulders are designed

for constant struggle.

Be as the stream, find your path, be gentle in your course.

At times a trickle, then, as the path widens,

allow your flow to run its course freely.

∞

5 July 2001

Stop talking and do it!

Your path awaits, fear not, your true

motivation leads you onward.

Let yourself ride the crest of the wave.

Find your way toward the top and look

upon all – what do you see?

From this vantage point many things become obvious.

Spread your wings, take flight,

for it is only through your faith

that your steps lead you homeward after all.

Do not be swayed by temptation,

for to allow your fears to take root and prosper,

is to become stagnant, out of flow, rhythm – out of step.

Challenge yourself daily, begin now.

What is your hunger? Where does it lead you?

Many hands caress, enfold, many voices ring, let yours.

Unbound your hands, your heart, your mind –

for it is not from here you will soar.

Freedom: is it a place, a time?

Allow the discovery to begin.

Human form awaits discovery,

remind yourself often,

ANAYAH JOI HOLILLY

test your truth,

ask yourself the question,

listen for the answer.

Do not hurry along.

Orchestration is not required,

the notes only need taking down as we speak them.

You are in the way of flow – remove desire, will,

yield to the Source – remember it

is not for you to conduct,

merely be available as the notes flow,

be washed, not yet, let go, or you will control nothing,

but loose your way toward the sunrise, and

be left only with the setting sun.

Spend some quiet time each day,

your path will appear to you refreshed and anew.

11 July 2001

Awaken, sleeping comes to its natural

conclusion for you soon,

for soon the sun will bring with its

warming rays a new message,

for your pathway is to be trodden in this light.

A shared message, the voices sing,

gather round, all intently await the news.

Bring forth the seeds. Scatter them wide.

Cast this way and that – allow the dispersal a wide arch.

Every corner, every one needs the news, glad tidings,

a must for aching hearts,

withered spirits – as a balm to a wound.

Caress the brows, let the hand be gentle, linger a moment.

The healing takes place in an instant for some –

never fear, the bonds are forged.

Tether not your voice to one language.

This gift knows not bounds of race, time, tide.

Crest the wave of choice –

A N A Y A H   J O I   H O L I L L Y

a remarkable event in itself,

hidden at times by doubt, for the moment only.

Allow the moment to pass, as pass it always does.

As with the stetting of the sun,

the valleys become blind to the horizon,

unable to confirm their existence,

but exist it does for those not needing the proof of sight,

but rather insight, being acceptable.

Nothing is lost to the eyes, for whether open or closed

the view remains unchanged, the truth remains revealed –

a revelation, as always to our knowingness, our trustingness,

our willingness to know truth, whatever the form

Wind your way ever onward,

allow the passage,

drink with delight.

8 August 2001

Reclaim only what belongs to you.

Leave all mementos where they belong –

with whom they belong to.

This path leads to clarity, to self.

An honest reflection is vital to your progress,

allow

alight

alarm may visit, receive it as you

would any welcome guest,

for with it comes opportunities,

enfold them with loving arms,

embrace the possibilities.

Many gifts await.

Open each and every memory with care and willingness,

be available to yourself, your inner self needs you now.

Allow discovery –

examine each new finding with care and concern,

for here you may find important news.

Think not on what you know.

Open the channels.

Even mighty rivers need the concourse, tributaries,

each leading to the other, till finally –

home, home to the Source –

each drop mingling with the other

each one reunited with its own kind –

family reunited as is necessary for the journey to have it's

beginning yet again

Ponder on this, for all is revealed in this by this.

Ring ...

she awaits, as do you.

The time is long overdue. Now is the time.

encourage one another -– each for the other,

relax the boundaries separating the two, it is time.

Open your arms –

welcome home, you two.

Listen – read between the lines, all

may not be apparent at first,

let the truth be unwoven from the everyday tapestry.

Unravel the 'yarn', listen carefully,

pay attention,

important revelations evolve.

Live long and prosper.

Live well and prosper.

∞

2 September 2001

Footsteps carry forth intentions, messages, promises,

not always bringing with them comfort.

In their wake, a lasting impression,

many whispers create tempo,

feel its rhythm, its chorus echo's with

the vibration of healing.

ANAYAH JOI HOLILLY

Immerse yourselves in the gentle lapping

of these waves, these echoes,

for from here is the proper place from

which to start your journey.

The train stops for all to board.

The opportunity exists for all.

As always, the choice belongs to you and you alone.

Welcome each new adventure as you

would an honoured friend,

for, it is from within these arms, that the

gift is found – that joy resides,

unbound – abounding, abiding

faith

hope

love

all are one after all –

they reside in the same possibility.

Unlock the door, open it wide, for it is

with the letting in of the light

that the answers come – they truly reside in the light.

Cast out shadows, flood the corners

with the healing power of light,

allow not the lingering of any shadow,

no matter how small, or insignificant,

it may seem to you at the time.

The dark has a way of creeping in

unnoticed, until once again,

the corners are places for secrets and

fables to weave half-truths,

to hide and bestow their patchwork of

lingering doubt on the living.

Break free

use your wings

take flight

leave this place behind you once and for all –

trust, trust, trust, this time.

This time – the time that is here and now.

Take it.

ANAYAH JOI HOLILLY

It belongs to you and you alone.

Break free.

∞

28 September 2001

Your path now becomes clearer – your will unbent, pliant,

a tool now, no longer a hindrance.

To use it is a gift, this will of yours, it

ploughs the fields, ready to be sewn.

Cultivate it, for to deny it is to waste this energy.

The motion it creates is to the good, for the good,

once it is no longer used against the flow, the rhythm.

A fork in the road around the bend –

life's twists and turns.

Seen from our perspective they are of

course merely a patchwork,

all woven together to make the most beautiful pattern –

each and every piece necessary, in

harmony with its neighbour.

Trust in us, allow us to be your guides.

All things, no matter how insignificant

it may seem to you,

is of course a stitch in the patchwork.

As in all things, be ever gentle, allow

the breath to continue,

for it is with this breath that not only

do you allow life to continue,

but also you allow us to weave our

love and light into your cloth –

this patchwork of wonder.

Such a glorious task it is for us, a labour

not, a joyous resonating of

purest love, energy, hope – forever moving forward,

forever winding its way on to you.

Shudder not, fear not, your time is at hand –

open your arms wide, you will need to stretch them wide,

for your bounty is great, remarkable,

remark upon this – here and there,

not to be denied, nor feared, for you have

seen, have you not, the need is great.

The human condition exists, it is true,

it is necessary –

but a part of the journey –

only a part, not to be confused with the journey itself.

All will find their way home, if the desire is great enough.

Sing, your vice is pure – you have seen this,

your treasure, your bounty to share, to cast wide –

not to be squandered, nor given favour among the few –

all have equal need – don't choose, leave such matters us.

The children will be sent to you –

His own little ones – they will come.

Fear not – fear will not nourish you,

you know this as the truth.

Time to allow all. Time to release.

You are not alone of course, a part – a part –

one part, needing its mate, its home among others.

Willingness – over shadows, overshadowed by fear.

Allow the fear, take flight,

our wings will carry you far and wide,

so easy for us – do not attempt it yourself,

we are available for this.

Open your hands, open your your heart, open your mind.

Cast your glance toward the horizon

for this is you are needed.

Take your place – or not, you alone must allow.

See the gentle curve of truth – feel its grace.

Know it

Speak it

Listen for it

Scatter it to the four winds – a blanket to

carry forward and wrap the weary in.

Time is – it just is, become – refuge is needed by many.

Earth Angels are required for this task.

As the winds carry forth the seeds of renewal,

so too are the Earth Angels necessary

to calm the lost children –

to undertake the task of showing the

possibilities – the choices –

for it is the choice, that is not realised by so many.

Choice needs to be offered before choice can be made.

Go forth – go home – go now, you know how,

you have the helpers available to you –

you have the Choice.

Make it

28 September 2001

Truck

crate

wings.

Important

Important

Be vigilant, cast your gaze to the horizon.

Wings will once again be needed, and provided.

You have seen this at work – easy – simple.

Be ready – coming to you now, so many voices –

sing, heed the harmony, the healing these tones bring

TRUST

TRUST

TRUST

US

∞

29 September 2001

The blankets are grey, their weave is coarse.

Draped across their shoulders, weary, fearful –

open your arms – open them wide,

so many many need holding.

Nurture – forge the bonds – their heads bend low.

Prevail, all will prevail.

Contact, Contact, it becomes more

necessary now, than ever before.

Like minds, soft hearts – shine – brilliant – beam –

radiance /radiant

Centre – gathering –

many souls find their way – a hearth

for the weary, hear the voices,

raise your own among them, be guided

December 2001

Willingness brings forth magic.

A new horizon, new beginnings.

Remember to open your mind, your heart, and your arms.

Folded arms are empty arms.

To carry abundance you must first throw

open your arms in welcome.

Beauty brings with it a paradox:

how to see the un-seeable.

First, you must close your eyes, then, open your heart.

Allow the well of insight to overflow, to

carry forth the true and beautiful you –

free of earthly restrictions, for the spirit that is truly you

carries with it no such deception, for

the beauty that is you, just is –

always unknowable to those whose eyes

remain focused on the physical alone.

Be still, be willing.

Your path is true - you only need be willing Cherub

∞

7 January 2002

Forceful – to force. To forge, see the difference?

Arrows pierce, cast them aside,

no good will come from competition.

Learn to bend gracefully, with grace,

for in grace, you will discover many strengths.

Allow

Alight

Alleviate

Your burdens crumble under the weight of

a simple smile, a thoughtful gesture.

You know this to be so –

so, sow as you intend to reap –

let the pain wash from your eyes and hearts –

allow this to be so; sow as you intend to reap.

Hark -little ones, do you hear the bells?

They ring for you.

Will you allow the tones to purify

your central nervous system?

For it is from here that you must

allow the healing to begin,

for in time, as you sow, so shall you reap.

Be careful – full of care – and quiet.

Measure your steps to fall not where

they may, but where they should.

Gossamer; fragile, yet forged for its strength

Remark – Remarkable

Yellow; remember Yellow when the time comes,

carries forth healing and awakening properties.

Joyous

Simple

go forth – dither not here and yonder.

ANAYAH JOI HOLILLY

Widen your window of opportunity by

selecting only positive influence,

with a single step, as all starts.

Willing hands await you.

Open the window child / many hearts need mending,

through ones hands, the window for healing,

a real possibility – forge ahead, your

plans bear many possibilities,

each one a pathway leading toward fruition

– each one –

The bells ring for you dear one, do you see?

Open your eyes, cast your glance this way and that,

Journey into the words whispered to me,

be willing and be free

allow

alight

a little goes a long way, crest the wave, look to the coast.

10 January 2002

Cast off your shackles

spin

turn

the planet vibrates, hums with energy,

willingness brings forth magic –

are you truly wiling?

float

feel.

17 January 2002

The truth seeks its path, the bends

and curves allow much to be

hidden from view, but nothing to be

so simple as to have no other

opportunity for growth.

ANAYAH JOI HOLILLY

Change – this way or that, abide by the truth at all costs,

for this is the way to the future you seek.

A powerful ally is truth.

Seek it

Guard it

Speak it

Whisper it

Allow it

for it is mighty – a power and a beauty in its own right.

Clear and true, like the wind, it

carries forth many changes.

Go with them, learn from them, abide

by them – your course is set.

Plot your course, follow the guide.

Look, do you see?

Do you feel the hands that guide you?

Stop and listen often, there is much

to hear, much to share.

Cast your net wide, what do you reap dear one?

A shallow dish holds its share of treasures –

empty the dish often, make way for the new.

Hold on to nothing, for in this way nothing

is all you will succeed in obtaining.

Scarcity is a state of mind, not a state of being,

for to be just is – be what you will –

for you will it to be so.

Allow abundance, truly it is there all the while,

available for those who see beyond the veil of fear –

fear not.

As you weave, be aware of the

transformation – of the process –

for it is the cloth of life that is

passing through your hands,

and as you add your texture to the weave,

you leave a blessing for those who follow in your wake.

Fear not precious one, you do no harm –

tis but a moment in time –

and as the moments blend, allow the

truth to dawn upon you:

though the spirit is willing, the hands

often times forget to weave –

but sooner, or later, the cloth is once again

taken up, and the weaving begins anew.

Tis the blanket for the weary, the weave

of love and comfort is indelible.

Cast it about the shoulders in times of trouble,

feel its gentle power, its soothing presence.

Each, and every soul. has at one time or

another, woven their magic into it –

its unity is its gift – not visible to the eyes of all,

but surely, to the hearts of the weary – of the wretched.

Carry it forth – offer it to one and all –

it only grows with use,

with its unfurling comes peace to all who wear it,

it will absorb the burdens of many, and grow

more beautiful for the experience,

its colours more vibrant and delicate at once.

Seek not wisdom –

for wisdom finds its way to you,

instead, be the seeker of truth.

Offer it as a balm for the weary of heart.

Be gentle; all children need to feel loving arms –

to see approval and love in the eyes of another,

reflecting back warmth and honour.

then this is turn will be mirrored onward –

and so it goes – from hand to hand –

each one leaving its bounty in the weave.

And as the cloth grows in beauty and size,

so too does its power, and healing.

Spread the cloth wide, leave not one corner unfurled.

17 January 2002

Be ready

the bells are ringing, they ring for you.

The time is here. and you are ready –

don't be afraid, your strength is abundant.

Tho your fear is great, your strength is greater.

One can indeed grow from the other, as you will see.

∞

17 January 2002

The events of September 11 have bought about change –

a change that is profound in the minds

and hearts of human beings –

truth is needed now as never before,

for many hundreds of thousands of human beings.

The Angel Thoughts need to be spread –

they are a blanket for the weary.

They offer hope, and a way of thinking,

so needed by so many.

Send them forth – seek the way – listen for the bells,

the ringing signals you are on the right path.

∞

18 January 2002

Be willing to be led, enjoy the journey,

for it is truly a beginning Cherub.

From the minds of man the thunder rolls, and

in its wake the destruction is savage.

Spread the cloth near and far, for even its

shadow has the power to heal –

many await its comfort.

Its true, judgement is easy, but a trap nonetheless,

for to judge is to invite judgement upon yourself.

ANAYAH JOI HOLILLY

It becomes obvious to those who wish to

embark upon their own journey,

that this is a useless endeavour, for you must

all put one foot in front of the other –

it is so, is it not?

Farewell the need to pick and choose.

Welcome your nurturing souls to join

together and become a brotherhood,

for it is in this way that the power lies.

Your family awaits – larger than you can imagine.

With your arms spread wide,

you will encompass humanity.

And so it is to be, a blessing to you

all, a wonder to behold.

Channel the message to all who would hear.

Do it now.

21 January 2002

Break free, run, dance, sing, your

moment has come pretty one.

9 February 2002

The bells ring for you –

remember this, tis our sign for your

recognition as time heals.

12 February 2002

The dance, the rhythm, its magic strums your heartstrings

creating a beauty and grace truly your own.

Sway in time, for in time your two hearts beat a chorus,

up lifting, up lifted, to soar above the

concerns of everyday life.

The rhythm is synchronised, for at this time of celebration

the bonds draw you near and dear – each to the other.

Tis a time of gentle discovery – believe in the truth of it –

believe in the clear waters that you now bathe in,

cast aside all trembling, all doubt – as

these do nothing to enhance

the beauty of this time that is upon you.

Wear the mantle of each soft caress,

hurry not, tread not with fear, but

with the sure footfalls of

a love in the birth of its wondrous beginnings,

of its tender shoots unfurling before the dawn

of this wondrous new beginning.

Allow each new day to dawn unclouded.

Arise anew.

20 February 2002

Release

renew

revive

all come from the one Source, as do all

the gifts channelled your way.

Allow the channel to grow ever wider.

Arrive/Arrival imminent,

be prepared, release, realise, real – ise do you see?

Lift the veil, cast it aside.

24 February 2002

The hour draws near, cast the net

wide, hands holding hearts.

Colour your world –

light the corners, for to you now

comes the way, the pathway.

Clear a space – make a place among the thorns.

Cultivate growth, Speake not – do – do now,

the momentum exists,

peruse it

harmonise

blend your essence with that of others

of like minds – gentle hearts,

strong hands carve the way forth.

Express the vision, soften the lines –merge – marry,

for the common good comes your

way an expression of hope –

renewal, repair all.

Such a time, this time of growth.

A resonance – sweet – pure, drink from the one Source –

drink deeply, sate your thirst, the well never runs dry.

Carmichael - remember the name in times to come.

Important, but not vital – resist.

The gentle curves need colour – allow it to be so.

∞

27 February 2002

Turn the pages –

the healing occurs for many in an instant,

for time is of no significance when the

healing energy is unbound.

Unfurl your wings

Take flight

Break free

Your pathway becomes clearer to you now,

you begin to see as we do,

the vision is vital, you have it, use it.

Illusions are useful tools – mock them not,

Allow the light to enter, it will lead you home.

Look to the elder for guidance on these matters –

your heart is tender Cherub, as it is meant to be,

but tend to it, allow not the heavy handed to bruise it.

Keep its delicate beat in Rhyme and Rhythm.

Its chambers contain a certain

magic – there for the dance.

Sway – feel the joy it brings?

Allow the rhythm, it has a beat all its

own – no drummer needed.

Gaze upon the world with thine own eyes –

taste its fruit with thine own lips – bitter or sweet.

Slayers not, menders all

– vital –

look to the centre, do not be swayed.

Open your arms – open them wide, accept one and all,

decipher the rhyme and reason as

you tread the winding road –

collect the silver with tenderness,

and gratitude, to one and all,

for from where does the sparrow come,

and to where does it fly?

Be true and just, the weary of heart seek the journeys end.

Raise your voice, let it ring true.

Offer the truth not less, soothe as

you would a young child,

calm, gentle.

Speake – US – the possibilities

Tis not the face but the beating heart

that resides within after all –

look to this place, and this place alone,

when in need of the truth.

∞

4 March 2002

Unravel the myth – for to you now

comes a journey – a pathway,

an adventure of a sort full of castles and queens,

with all the magic, and around which your footsteps echo.

Sway in time – allow the rhythm to

encircle your hearts and minds.

ANAYAH JOI HOLILLY

Allow the creation to flow forth –

within the mighty beats a tender heart.

Unbend your will, allow,

bonds forged – hearts mended – like minds, open arms.

Cast the yellow stone –

weigh the cost, for a cost is applied to all Choice

Wander not, stay.

Apply.

Work, as you know you must – for the greater good.

Plant, nourish – reap; how else is the cycle to be?

Did you truly expect it any other way?

Look at the leaves as they fall,

allow each one to reside where they may.

To the casual glance, merely a carpet of

leaves – discord among the order.

Look ever closer. What do you see?

It is there, a perfectly layered existence.

Scattered, cast asunder, the form once

so perfect, now a thing apart,

each part lost to the other – each

partnership without its echo.

One without the other.

Merely an opportunity for growth missed?

For a new element denied the chance to flourish?

And your layers?

Nurtured, or swept aside? A place of opportunity,

or a dank, and dismal place, for the sweetness to be lost?

7 March 2002

The well never runs dry – not ever.

Can you imagine this?

For truly it is so – a never-ending spring of possibilities,

of hope, of renewal

Imagine us – we watch you play, fall, pick yourselves up,

ANAYAH JOI HOLILLY

and run again.

Forever onwards, forever learning.

It is as it should be – was always meant to be.

Hurry not, for in haste chances are

missed, the way easily mistaken

mis – taken

think on this, ponder at length.

Allow the time for your conscious mind

to wander this way and that –

all is remembered – though not easily accessed by your

waking memory – tis there though.

Shortness of breath is not wise,

not a matter to be hurried past, hurried through.

Wander along each and every pathway.

Stop often – reflect.

Allow the minds eye to turn toward the centre, to linger.

No harm will come from this,

rather, notice as you pass each string – how finely tuned is it?

Will the music be sweet when strummed?

The hearts yearnings for harmony,

requires each and every string

to be touched with loving thoughts,

gentle hands, a caress. Pluck them with tenderness,

allow the melody – allow it to ring true and clear.

No reason for fear, for all is possible when

loving arms are open in welcome.

Feel their grace – know this is where

home is – where comfort resides.

Light the fires – mark the way – mark time.

Find the beat – walk within it.

Run not ahead, lag not behind.

The tuning is a thing of beauty,

allow yourself the power it brings.

Slumber has past.

Gather your resources, marshal your

talents, pool your wealth,

your talents, for they are one and the

same, each akin to the other.

A N A Y A H   J O I   H O L I L L Y

The beauty is there – look and it opens before you.

It was there all the while – waiting patiently.

Lilly pads – look for them – remark upon them,

a small sign, but a sign nonetheless.

The water soothes – mends, brings comfort.

Little footsteps echo – echoes ring, linger, as do whispers.

A word here, a touch there.

Spread the cloth, cast it wide.

A new day dawns.

Greet the sunrise,

Turn your face toward the light.

8 March 2002

An ocean lapping, its warm currents greet you,

enfold you, rock you in its gentle arms.

Feel its Rhythm, it soothes, offers hope.

Delight in it. feel it enfold you, rock you like a babe in arms, dance with you held, oh so gently.

The heart warms, the glow spreads,

reaches each and every corner.

Feel it play about your lips – the bow curves,

the hope

the joy

the radiance spills from the corners,

(Bellsong – Remember this –

the Bells ring for you, for each and every one of you)

trickles out into the world, there for all to see –

for those that do, truly do – will treasure this moment,

will replay it often, allow it as a balm –

as of course it is intended to be.

And as it makes its way out into the world,

it brings forth an even greater gift:

opportunity – for each eye that beholds its sweetness,

for each heart that yields to its beckoning,

will in turn, have the opportunity to spill its

own sweetness into the world.

∞

12 March 2002

Home coming – a journey of many roads, many detours,

yet all roads do lead you home.

Do you see the beauty of it all?

Winding or straight, what a joyous event,

for no pathway leads the child far from loving arms.

Become still, for in the stillness the whispers are heard –

recognised, allowed.

Hear them – what is their message to you?

For a message comes upon each and every soft breath.

It is there – residing in the quiet.

Hush now, be open and willing to

the words of hope and truth.

Hear them – fear them – tis but a

state of perception after all.

Adapt, for here lies strength.

∞

17 March 2002

Seekers of truth, willing ears,

loving hands, the circle begun.

The quest, the journey, fables not, menders all.

Join your hands, your hearts,

for this quest is the road you seek –

the journeys end ends not,

weaves its magic into the cloth –

the wisdom will come – a little at a time.

Patience, patience, one foot in front of the other –

this is the way, the truth lies here. Many seek it,

bathe their wounds in it – with it, anoint their battered souls,

untangle their wings – they too need to take flight.

Cast the yellow stone – each truth – each

question asked, honour them all.

For the undertaking never sleeps.

Sooth the fears, dry the tears.

ANAYAH JOI HOLILLY

The children come to you –

gather them close, observe the hush,

the quiet carries many echoes.

Reflection is vital to the outcome, for one, for all.

Footsore and weary they come, their eyes downcast.

∞

17 March 2002

To you, now comes.

Celebrate!

On wings of truth and honour, comes

to you the opportunity for

growth and freedom.

As a *rose bud, your time for gentle unfurling takes place.

When the heart is willing, the instruction awaits –

gentle hearts willing hands

[*see 27 March 2001 pertaining to this point]

∞

27 March 2002

Allow not the time to slip by unheeded,

for it is within this passage of time,

that your possibilities flow.

Hark

heed

around the corner comes to you, the

why and the wherefore,

time to pay attention, dally not,

tis wise to focus your energies with precision.

more care full attention is needed.

Bring the group together tell them – one and all –

to cast the yellow stone, to flood the corners with light.

The one necessary to the project is not at hand

cast, look, listen, they will come.

Opportunities abound – you know this, let it be so,

fight not the flow – seek to mend, to dry the tears.

Harsh words spoken cast a stone in the heart,

its weight often forgotten, but there all the same –

weighty – hurting.

Seek to remove it, to repair.

All roads lead home – the passage paid,

the fare affordable.

You have your ticket, your passport, many stamps await.

Just allow, it comes to you, you need not seek.

All for its purpose, all in time, as in

time, flows to you, the journey,

the momentum plays it rhythm, strums its own chord,

of its own accord.

Listen, you will hear it winding its way to you.

Its wings beat in time, your heart

murmurs, whispers, then sings.

Allow the notes to ring pure and true.

Laugh in gay abandon, feel its power surge

forth, cleansing, as truth is prone to do.

Be ready – the time is now now now,

light the fires – mark the way.

Yellow.

A simple truth – it has its own power, its own beauty is

there all the while, look, allow, be truth in all things.

Happiness grows from the smallest seeds –

nurture them, allow their roots to take hold.

Feel them gently take hold, remember

to shower them in golden light.

Nurture them always in the gentle mist – not of tears,

but of laughter, joy, tenderness,

displayed to those you encounter, and as you do,

rejoice, for it is your Fathers work you do.

His greatest gift to you, your tender heart, sweet and pure,

love of your fellow man.

Not all share in your joy tis true, but

let it be enough that you do,

but – mend your own fences first!

For how else can it be Cherub, tenderness is your tool,

ANAYAH JOI HOLILLY

use it wisely, use it well,

use it – not sparingly, but lavishly, with gay abandon.

Let the trickle become the stream, let

the stream become the river,

the river become the ocean,

there to bathe in, to float upon, to delight in,

to rock and comfort you, one, and

all, rock you oh so gently,

with a tenderness so enriching as to

be almost heartbreaking.

For the heart is the doorway in.

Open it, open it wide, flood the world with its magic,

one and all, for here lies the slayers of secrets, of fables,

the way to truth, freedom, home.

Let the mending begin

MORE MESSAGES TO COME

Remember your magnificence.

Divine Assignments

A message to you from your loving angels

We implore you to you to Ask! Ask! Ask!

Have you asked us for our assistance

today, yesterday, last week?

For more peace, more love, more money, more assistance,

help to experience more feelings of joy and balance?

We are here to guide you to ask for more, to

take this important step without delay.

This is not a sign of weakness, nor of greed

dear one, rather a sign of faith and prosperity.

It is all yours for the asking. Ask for more!

We are waiting for your invitation. We

have much to share with you.

Begin by asking for *yourself*, this is important,

and not to be underestimated.

Love, your angels.

ANAYAH JOI HOLILLY

Ask us to bring you whatever it is you desire, need or want. It is important to begin your Divine Assignments by asking for *yourself* first. Begin asking now, it's an important step for you. Remember, even baby steps count.

1.

2.

3.

4.

5.

Please speak these words as prayer:

"Today I ask and invite you my loving

angels to bring me clarity about..."

1.

2.

3.

4.

5.

∞

Ask for blessings for your family, for your loved ones. No matter what has gone before, allow it to rest, and ask for love and blessing for each person.

1.

2.

3.

4.

5.

6.

7.

8.

9.

10.

*Continue in a note book, or journal, if

you need more space, and as you

think of, or feel, more names 'pop' into your awareness.

Ask for blessings for Governments, for policy makers.

1.

2.

3.

4.

5.

*Remember, feeling anger and resentment

toward governments will not bring

about peace, love, compassion, or wisdom – for anyone.

Ask for your community, your town.

Continue on a separate sheet as your

inspiration flows, now, or at any time in the future.

1.

2.

3.

4.

5.

∞

Ask for your country, and the people of your country.

1.

2.

3.

5.

ANAYAH JOI HOLILLY

Ask for specific blessings for decision
makers in Corporations

1.

2.

3.

5.

∞

Please say out loud:

"Today I ask and invite you my loving

angels, to help and guide me with..."

1.

2.

3.

4.

5.

*You can never ask too often, or for too much.

We have all the time in the world for you

our dear one. And then some.

∞

ANAYAH JOI HOLILLY

Ask for blessings for specific countries,

and for all people of that country:

1.

2.

3.

4.

5.

∞

List 5 things, 5 people, or situations, you
are grateful for right now, and why.
This time honoured way of expressing
gratitude, is a powerful support.

1.

2.

3.

5.

∞

ANAYAH JOI HOLILLY

Ask for at least 2 blessings for someone who irritates you.

You can add more any time.

1.

2.

3.

4.

5.

∞

Ask for blessings for your neighbours.

1.

2.

3.

5.

∞

Ask for animals, nature, the oceans, the atmosphere.

1.

2.

ANAYAH JOI HOLILLY

3.

5.

∞

List 5 events, or 5 people who have helped

you in some unexpected way.

1.

2.

3.

5.

∞

List at least 2 blessings for someone you
feel anger, or resentment toward.
You can add more any time.

1.

2.

3.

4.

5.

∞

List at least 5 things/qualities you love,

value and appreciate about yourself.

Take a breath, and take this important step.

There is no need to rush this, but please,

write at least one before you move on, even

if it makes you feel uncomfortable.

All change begins with courage.

1.

2.

3.

4.

5.

∞

There are obvious ways to feel grateful and blessed.

List some ways that may not be immediately apparent to you.

Be willing to sit with this if you need to.

1.

2.

3.

4.

5.

∞

List a blessing COVID-19 has revealed, or is revealing

in some way, for yourself or others.

ANAYAH JOI HOLILLY

*We do understand this may be extremely challenging,
particularly if a loved one has chosen to depart their
physical body. Yet, the power of love exits in everything,
every moment, and in everyone. You
are strong, brave and beautiful.

Come back to this one if you need to. We
only ask that you ponder on it.

1.

2.

3.

4.

5.

∞

Congratulations!

You are learning the gifts of asking, and

of recognising blessings in disguise.

We applaud you!

Ask us for assistance with everything, no

matter how large, how seemingly small,

or insignificant your need, or your question, may

seem to you. We love and value you, and it is our joy

to assist, and guide you – always and in all ways.

Please talk to us every day.

Remember, there are no limits to our love

for you, nor to your magnificence!

Your loving angels

ANAYAH JOI HOLILLY

GLOSSARY

Here are some of the words the angels use throughout *The Angel Code* that you may not be familiar with, in no particular order.

Your time is at hand = your time is arriving, it is almost time, unfolding in its perfect moment, i.e. in Divine Timing

Abound = To be in a state of great plenty, to be or feel rich in something, to flourish

Alight = provided with light/land/(of a bird) descend from the air and settle

Align = Adjust, come into alignment with

Forge = (in this case) to advance

Cherub = a beautiful and innocent person. [When we are addressed as Cherub, it is to signify the angels reminding us we are beautiful and innocent in truth, in spirit, no matter what we have done, seen, or thought, this is who we remain in our Creators, and therefore, in the angels, eyes,]

Chide = criticise, rebuke, give yourself a 'hard time' over something

Biding = continuing, remain/remaining

Fraught = full of (as in fraught with danger)/upset/tense/ on edge over something

Sate = to satisfy til full.

Course = option/choice/advance in a particular direction/ the path, route or channel along which anything moves/ advance in a particular direction/ regular or natural order of events.

Forged = (**Forge**) to form or make in any way.

Abounding = abundant/abundance

Hark = listen/listen to

Take heed = pay careful attention,

Tidings = News, information, communication

Unbound = unchained, free/free from, the angels may also use this word to express their guidance to us to release something, ideas, outdated beliefs and actions etc.

Share your experience #TheAngelCodeBook

Printed in the USA
CPSIA information can be obtained
at www.ICGtesting.com
LVHW091613150224
771928LV00032B/105